DATE DUE

PowerKids Readers:

The Bilingual Library of the
United States of America™

MICHIGAN

JOSÉ MARÍA OBREGÓN

TRADUCCIÓN AL ESPAÑOL: MARÍA CRISTINA BRUSCA

The Rosen Publishing Group's
PowerKids Press™ & **Editorial Buenas Letras**™
New York

Bilingual Edition
English/Spanish
Edición bilingüe

Published in 2006 by The Rosen Publishing Group, Inc.
29 East 21st Street, New York, NY 10010

First Edition

Book Design: Albert B. Hanner
Photo Credits: Cover, pp. 5, 30 (The Great Lakes State, The Wolverine State) Albert B. Hanner; pp. 7, 31 (Border, Peninsula) © 2002 Geoatlas; pp. 9, 30 (state motto) © William Manning/Corbis; p. 11 © Layne Kennedy/Corbis; p. 13 © Corbis; pp. 15, 19, 31(Pontiac, Edison, Ford, Louis) © Bettmann/Corbis; 17 © Library of Congress Prints and Photographs Division; pp. 21, 26, 30 (apple blossom) © Royalty-Free/Corbis; p. 23 © Todd Gipstein/Corbis; pp. 25, 30 (capital) © Joseph Sohm; Chromosohm Inc./Corbis; p. 30 (Robin) © Tim Wright/Corbis; p. 30 (White Pine) © Richard Hamilton Smith/Corbis; p. 31 (bald eagle) © Pete Saloutos/Corbis; p. 31 (herd) © Tom Brakefield/Corbis; p. 31 (Madonna) © Mitchell Gerber/Corbis; p. 31 (Magic Johnson) © Neal Preston/Corbis

Library of Congress Cataloging-in-Publication Data

Obregón, José María, 1963–
Michigan / José María Obregón ; traducción al español, María Cristina Brusca.— 1st ed.
p. cm. — (The bilingual library of the United States of America) English and Spanish.
Includes bibliographical references and index.
ISBN 1-4042-3087-4 (library binding)
1. Michigan—Juvenile literature. I. Title. II. Series.
F566.3.O27 2006
977.4—dc22
                              2005008354

Manufactured in the United States of America

Due to the changing nature of Internet links, Editorial Buenas Letras has developed an online list of Web sites related to the subject of this book. This site is updated regularly. Please use this link to access the list:

http://www.buenasletraslinks.com/ls/michigan

Contents

Contenido

Welcome to Michigan

These are the flag and seal of the state of Michigan. A bald eagle is in the center of the seal. The bald eagle is the national bird of the United States.

Bienvenidos a Michigan

Estos son la bandera y el escudo del estado de Michigan. En el centro del escudo hay un águila calva. El águila calva es el ave nacional de los Estados Unidos.

E PLURIBUS UNUM

TUEBOR

SI QUAERIS PENINSULAM AMOENAM

CIRCUMSPICE

THE GREAT SEAL OF THE STATE OF MICHIGAN

E PLURIBUS UNUM

TUEBOR

SI QUAERIS PENINSULAM AMOENAM

CIRCUMSPICE

A.D. MDCCCXXXV.

Michigan Flag and State Seal

Bandera y escudo de Michigan

Michigan Geography

Michigan borders the states of Ohio, Wisconsin, and Indiana, and the country of Canada. Michigan is made up of two peninsulas. A peninsula is a piece of land that is almost completely surrounded by water.

Geografía de Michigan

Michigan linda con los estados de Ohio, Indiana y Wisconsin y con el país de Canadá. Michigan está formado por dos penínsulas. Una península es una porción de tierra que está casi completamente rodeada de agua.

Isle Royal
Isla Royal

Lake Superior
Lago Superior

CANADA
CANADÁ

Sault Sainte Marie ●

Mackinaw City ●

Beaver Island
Isla Beaver

Lake Huron
Lago Hurón

WISCONSIN

● Traverse City

Muskegon River
Río Muskegon

MICHIGAN

Flint River
Río Flint

● Flint

Map Key
Claves del mapa

● Major City
   Ciudad principal

⭐ Capital
   Capital

River
Río

● Grand Rapids

Lake Michigan
Lago Michigan

Lansing ⭐

Detroit ●

Lake Erie
Lago Erie

Map of Michigan

Mapa de Michigan

ILLINOIS

OHIO

INDIANA

Michigan is surrounded by four of the Great Lakes. These lakes are the largest in the United States. They are Lake Superior, Lake Huron, Lake Erie, and Lake Michigan.

Michigan está rodeado por cuatro de los Grandes Lagos. Estos lagos son los más grandes de los Estados Unidos. Se llaman lago Superior, lago Hurón, lago Erie y lago Michigan.

Lake Michigan

Lago Michigan

Isle Royale is the only national park in Michigan. It is made of one main island and around 200 small islands. Isle Royale is home to the largest herd of moose in the United States.

La isla Royale es el único parque nacional de Michigan. Está compuesto por una isla principal y alrededor de 200 islas pequeñas. La isla Royale es el hogar de la manada de alces más grande de los Estados Unidos.

Moose in Isle Royale

Alce en la isla Royale

Michigan History

The name Michigan comes from the Native American word *michigama*. It means "great lake." The Ojibwa, Menoninee, Miami, Wyandot, and other Native Americans have lived in Michigan for thousands of years.

Historia de Michigan

El nombre Michigan viene de la palabra indígena michigama, que significa "lago grande". Las tribus Ojibwa, Menoninee, Miami, Wyandot y otras tribus nativoamericanas han vivido en Michigan por miles de años.

Ojibwa Warriors Perform a War Dance

Guerreros Ojibwa bailando una danza guerrera

In 1668, a French explorer and priest named Jacques Marquette built the first European settlement in Michigan. The French named the settlement Sault Sainte Marie.

En 1668, un sacerdote y explorador francés, llamado Jacques Marquette, construyó la primera población europea en Michigan. Los franceses llamaron a esta población Sault Sainte Marie.

Father Jacques Marquette

El padre Jacques Marquette

Michigan became the twenty-sixth state of the Union in 1837. Stevens T. Mason was elected the first state governor. Mason was only 25 years old.

En 1837, Michigan se convirtió en el estado veintiseis de la Unión. Stevens T. Mason fue elegido primer gobernador del estado. Mason tenía solamente veinticinco años.

Stevens T. Mason

Henry Ford was born on a Michigan farm in 1863. When he was 40 years old he founded the Ford Motor Company in Michigan. In 1913, he invented the Model T. This is one of the most famous cars in history.

Henry Ford nació en una granja de Michigan en 1863. Cuando tenía 40 años fundó la Companía Ford en Michigan. En 1913, Ford inventó el Modelo T. Éste es uno de los automóviles más famosos de la historia.

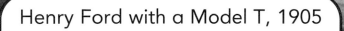

Henry Ford with a Model T, 1905
___

Henry Ford en un Modelo T, en 1905

Living in Michigan

Detroit is the largest city in Michigan. Detroit is known as Motor City. This is because Detroit is famous for making cars. Many big car factories are located around Detroit.

La vida en Michigan

Detroit es la ciudad más grande de Michigan. Detroit es conocida como la Ciudad del Automóvil porque es famosa por fabricar autos. Muchas grandes fábricas de automóviles están en los alrededores de Detroit.

Detroit Skyline

Vista de la ciudad de Detroit

Traverse City, Michigan, is known as the Cherry Capital of the World. Each July the city holds the National Cherry Festival. Thousands of people from all over the world visit Traverse City. They enjoy the festival and eat cherries.

Traverse City, Michigan, es conocida como la Capital Mundial de la Cereza. En julio, la ciudad celebra el Festival nacional de la cereza. Miles de personas de todo el mundo visitan Traverse City. Los visitantes disfrutan del festival y de las cerezas.

Sorting Cherries in Traverse City, Michigan

Escogiendo cerezas en Traverse City, Michigan

Detroit, Grand Rapids, Warren, Flint, and Lansing are important cities in Michigan. Lansing is the capital of the state.

Detroit, Grand Rapids, Warren, Flint y Lansing son ciudades importantes de Michigan. Lansing es la capital del estado.

State Capitol Building in Lansing, Michigan

Capitolio del estado en Lansing, Michigan

Activity:
Let's Draw Michigan's State Flower

The apple blossom became Michigan's state flower in 1897

Actividad:
Dibujemos la flor del estado de Michigan

La flor del manzano es la flor del estado de Michigan desde 1897

1

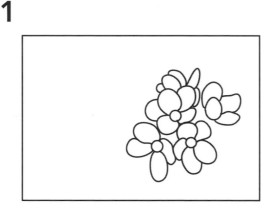

Draw a rectangle. Inside the rectangle draw three small circles for the inside of the blossoms. Then draw the petals around the circles. Add some more petals.

Dibuja un rectángulo. Adentro del rectángulo traza tres pequeños círculos para hacer el centro de las flores. Luego dibuja los pétalos alrededor de los círculos. Agrega algunos pétalos más.

2

Draw the branch and the leaves surrounding the apple blossoms.

Dibuja la rama y las hojas que rodean a las flores.

3

Now draw the small buds that have not yet bloomed near the top.

Ahora, cerca de la parte de arriba, dibuja las pequeñas yemas que no han florecido todavía.

4

Now shade the apple blossom drawing.

Ahora sombrea el dibujo de las flores.

Timeline Cronología

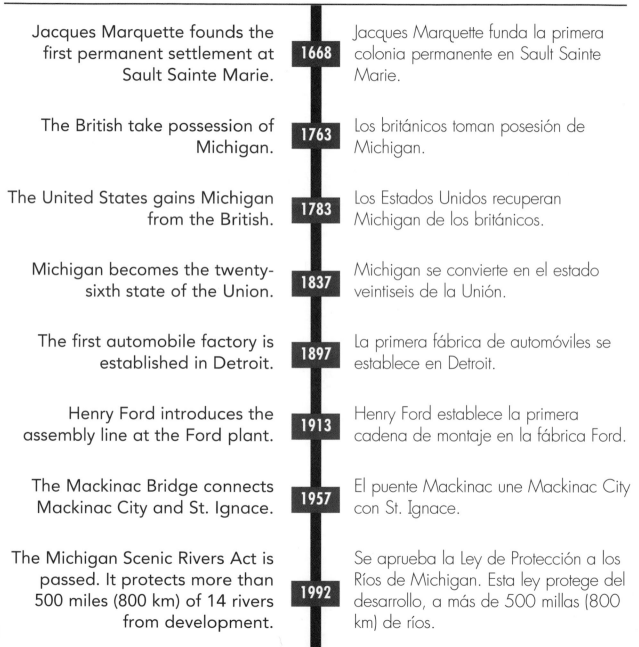

1668
Jacques Marquette founds the first permanent settlement at Sault Sainte Marie.

Jacques Marquette funda la primera colonia permanente en Sault Sainte Marie.

1763
The British take possession of Michigan.

Los británicos toman posesión de Michigan.

1783
The United States gains Michigan from the British.

Los Estados Unidos recuperan Michigan de los británicos.

1837
Michigan becomes the twenty-sixth state of the Union.

Michigan se convierte en el estado veintiseis de la Unión.

1897
The first automobile factory is established in Detroit.

La primera fábrica de automóviles se establece en Detroit.

1913
Henry Ford introduces the assembly line at the Ford plant.

Henry Ford establece la primera cadena de montaje en la fábrica Ford.

1957
The Mackinac Bridge connects Mackinac City and St. Ignace.

El puente Mackinac une Mackinac City con St. Ignace.

1992
The Michigan Scenic Rivers Act is passed. It protects more than 500 miles (800 km) of 14 rivers from development.

Se aprueba la Ley de Protección a los Ríos de Michigan. Esta ley protege del desarrollo, a más de 500 millas (800 km) de ríos.

Michigan Events

Eventos en Michigan

Michigan Events	Eventos en Michigan
February I-500 Snowmobile Race in Sault Sainte Marie	**Febrero** Carrera de motonieve I-500, en Sault Sainte Marie
March Invitational Nordic Ski Race in Newberry	**Marzo** Carrera abierta de esquí nórdico, en Newberry
May Grand Prix in Detroit	**Mayo** Gran premio de Detroit
June Cereal Festival in Battle Creek	**Junio** Festival del cereal, en Battle Creek
July National Cherry Festival in Traverse City International Cherry Pit Spitting Championship in Eau Claire	**Julio** Festival nacional de la cereza, en Traverse City Campeonato internacional de escupida de la semilla de la cereza, en Eau Claire
August Upper Peninsula State Fair in Escanaba State Fair in Detroit	**Agosto** Feria estatal de la península superior, en Escanaba Feria del estado, en Detroit
October Fall Colors, statewide	**Octubre** Colores del otoño, en todo el estado
December Christmas at Greenfield Village in Dearborn	**Diciembre** Navidad en Greenfield Village, en Dearborn

Michigan Facts/Datos sobre Michigan

Population
9.9 million

Población
9.9 millones

Capital
Lansing

Capital
Lansing

State Motto
If you seek a pleasant peninsula look about you

Lema del estado
Si buscas una península placentera, mira a tu alrededor

State Flower
Apple Blossom

Flor del estado
Flor del manzano

State Bird
Robin

Ave del estado
Petirrojo

State Nickname
The Great Lakes State,
The Wolverine State

Mote del estado
El Estado de Los Grandes Lagos, El Estado del Glotón

State Tree
White Pine

Árbol del estado
Pino blanco

State Song
"Michigan, My Michigan"

Canción del estado
"Michigan, mi Michigan"

Famous Michiganders/Michiguenses famosos

Pontiac
(1720–1769)

Indian leader
Líder indio

Thomas Edison
(1847–1931)

Inventor
Inventor

Henry Ford
(1863–1947)

Industrialist
Empresario

Joe Louis
(1914–1981)

Boxer
Boxeador

Madonna
(1958–   )

Singer, actress
Cantante, actriz

Magic Johnson
(1959–   )

Basketball player
Jugador de baloncesto

Words to Know/Palabras que debes saber

bald eagle
águila calva

border
frontera

herd
manada

peninsula
península

Here are more books to read about Michigan:
Otros libros que puedes leer sobre Michigan:

In English/En inglés:

My First Book About Michigan
The Michigan Experience
by Marsh, Carole
Gallopade International, 2000

Michigan
America the Beautiful
by Hintz, Martin
Children's Press, 1998

Words in English: 342

Palabras en español: 349

Index

Índice